PONDERING AND PRAYING VATICAN II

Coordinated by Elaine Penrice fsp
Graphic design, typeset and photographs by Ewa Głowińska fsp
except the following photographs: Sergia Ballini fsp (p. 40, 49),
Pauline Archive (p. 12, 16, 17, 20, 21, 22, 28, 37, 46, 58, 60, 80),
Cover photo: St Peter's Square © Dan / Adobe Stock.

Page 14: Altar of the Dormition of the Blessed Virgin Mary, Wit Stwosz, St. Mary's Basilica in Kraków, Poland
Page 64: Via della Conciliazione with a view of St. Peter's Basilica, Rome, Italy

ISBN 978-19-04785-84-2

Pauline

BOOKS & MEDIA

84 Church Street
Liverpool
L1 3AY

Pauline Books & Media is an expression of the ministry of the Daughters of St Paul, a charity registered in England and Wales under ref 296042 and in Scotland under ref SC 037889

Printed by **Gutenberg Press Ltd,** Gudja Road, Tarxien GXQ 2902 Malta

PONDERING AND PRAYING VATICAN II

JOHN WILSON

Archbishop John Wilson was ordained a priest for the Diocese of Leeds in 1995. He was ordained an Auxiliary Bishop in the Diocese of Westminster in 2016 and appointed Archbishop of Southwark in 2019.

CONTENTS

INTRODUCING VATICAN II

Have you heard about Vatican II, and want to know more, but are not sure where or how to begin? Then this little introduction is for you. It will help you start a journey of discovery by pondering and praying some essential themes. Please do not be daunted. This resource requires no previous or specialist knowledge. It has been written for easy access to what the Church said at Vatican II, and what this means for our life of faith in the Body of Christ.

BASICS ABOUT VATICAN II

The ***Second Ecumenical Vatican Council***, often referred to as Vatican II, was a remarkable event in the worldwide Catholic Church. The Council was called by Pope John XXIII to enable the Church to meet the missionary demands of proclaiming the Gospel.

Vatican II began on 11 October 1962 in St Peter's Basilica, Rome. Over 4000 bishops from across the world gathered there with the Pope. They met in four autumn sessions, across the following years, concluding on 8 December 1965. Having opened the Council, Pope John XXIII died in June 1963. It was, therefore, his successor Pope Paul VI who continued, and then concluded, Vatican II. Both popes were later declared saints, St John XXIII in 2014 and St Paul VI in 2018, in recognition of their holiness in imitating Christ.

It is often said that Vatican II sought an *aggiornamento* in the life and mission of the Church. This is the Italian word for 'an updating.' It speaks of the need to be equipped for evangelisation in every age, always faithful to the guidance of the Holy Spirit and the commission of the Lord Jesus to *'go and make disciples.' (Mt 28:19)* Another word used in relation to Vatican II is the French word *ressourcement* which means 'a return to the sources.' It refers to the desire to ground the Church's thinking more clearly in the Scriptures and the Church Fathers, the Christian writers of the early centuries of the Church.

THE DOCUMENTS OF VATICAN II

Through prayerful discernment, discussion, and drafting of texts, the bishops at Vatican II approved sixteen documents, often referred to as the *Documents of Vatican II*. Foundational to these are the four ***Constitutions*** which explain important dimensions of Catholic faith:

The **Constitution on the Sacred Liturgy** (4 Dec 1963) - about how we worship

The **Dogmatic Constitution on the Church** (21 Nov 1964) - about what it means to be the Body of Christ

The **Dogmatic Constitution on Divine Revelation** (18 Nov 1965) - about how God speaks to us

The **Pastoral Constitution on the Church in the Modern World** (7 Dec 1965) – about the relationship of the Church to contemporary social and global matters

Two of these ***Constitutions*** are called *dogmatic*, from the Greek word 'dogma' meaning belief or conviction. These express important teachings held by the Church. Another Constitution is called *pastoral*, from the Latin word 'pastor' meaning shepherd. It refers to how, following the example of Christ, the Good Shepherd, we reach out to each other and the world. All the documents were originally written in Latin and then translated into many different languages.

Along with the four ***Constitutions***, Vatican II also produced other important documents: on mass media, Eastern Catholic Churches, relations with other Christians (ecumenism), bishops, religious life, priestly formation, Christian education, relations with people of other religious beliefs (interreligious dialogue), the laity, religious freedom, missionary activity and the ministry and life of priests. These are all available to read, in both full and summary format, in print and on the internet.

UNDERSTANDING VATICAN II

Although many people have heard of Vatican II, few have actually read or considered the documents, not even the four key Constitutions. This resource offers an introduction to these main texts and their themes. It is not an extensive theological or historical assessment. These are certainly available for anyone who wants them. Rather, think of these pages more like the taster for a banquet, bite-sized nibbles which give just a flavour of something much greater.

Hopefully, ***Pondering and Praying Vatican II*** will encourage more people to read the full documents for themselves. Significantly, it will help readers ask themselves what the teaching of the Second Vatican Council might mean for them and how they might pray in light of it. Anyone can begin these reflections and see where the journey leads.

TITLES AND ABBREVIATIONS

It is helpful to know that the documents of Vatican II are often referred to by their title in Latin. This is usually the first two or three words of the opening sentence in the original Latin text. So, for example, the *Constitution on the Church* is also called *Lumen Gentium ('light of the nations'*) because the Latin opening sentence begins *Lumen gentium cum sit Christus* which translates as *'Christ is the light of nations.'* When referenced, these titles are usually abbreviated. So, *Lumen Gentium* becomes *LG* and the number which follows refers to the paragraph number, not the page number.

USING THIS RESOURCE

This resource can be used by individuals, working each day or week through the different sections related to the four Constitutions, taking time to reflect and pray. It can also be used by a group of people who might want to reflect together across a number of meetings, sharing their responses and prayer.

So, there you have it; enough to make a start. There is so much that can be said about Vatican II, and so much that has been written. You can continue to deepen your understanding if you are interested. Here we will consider simple summaries of the themes from the four Constitutions to help our **understanding.** Then there are some questions for **reflection** which point us to **prayer**.

INVOKING THE HOLY SPIRIT

Throughout the Church's history different gatherings, at Councils and Synods, have opened with a prayer to the Holy Spirit attributed to St Isidore of Seville (b. 560 d. 636). This same prayer was also used at the beginning of every session of the Second Vatican Council.

The prayer is called *Adsumus, Sancte Spiritus* from the opening words in Latin which translate *'We stand before you Holy Spirit.'* You might want to offer this prayer at the beginning of each time of reflection, either personally or within a group.

We stand before you, Holy Spirit,
as we gather together in your name.
With you alone to guide us,
make yourself at home in our hearts;
Teach us the way we must go
and how we are to pursue it.
We are weak and sinful;
do not let us promote disorder.
Do not let ignorance lead us down the wrong path
nor partiality influence our actions.
Let us find in you our unity
so that we may journey together to eternal life
and not stray from the way of truth
and what is right.
All this we ask of you,
who are at work in every place and time,
in the communion of the Father and the Son,
forever and ever. Amen.

"The four Constitutions of the Second Vatican Ecumenical Council, together with the Magisterium of these recent decades, will continue to provide direction and guidance to God's holy people, so that it can press forward in its mission of bringing the joyful proclamation of the Gospel to everyone."

Pope Francis, Letter for the Jubilee Year 2025, 11 February 2022

WORSHIP THE LORD IN THE SPLENDOUR OF HOLINESS.

PSALM 96:9

PART 1

THE LITURGY

THE COUNCIL AND THE LITURGY

(SC 1 – 4)

UNDERSTANDING

Vatican II's *Constitution on the Sacred Liturgy* was issued solemnly on 4 December 1963. It is often referred to as *Sacrosanctum Concilium* from the opening words of the original Latin text which translate as *'This Sacred Council...'* It is abbreviated as SC.
The bishops at Vatican II desired to increase the vitality and dynamism of Christian discipleship; to foster unity among Christians; and to call people to greater belonging to the Church. The renewal and revision of the liturgy was seen as essential to all of this.
Liturgy is the public worship and prayer of the Church. By participating in the liturgy, God's people celebrate the salvation Christ gained for us by his death and resurrection. It is through the liturgy, through our worship and prayers - and especially through the Eucharist and other sacraments - that we share and experience the mystery and reality of Christ's life in the Church. Our visible human celebrations connect us to the invisible divine truths of our faith. Celebrating the liturgy, faithful to tradition, helps us grow in faith and unity. It strengthens us to witness to Christ and serve him in our world.

REFLECTION

In what ways is the liturgy important to your life as a disciple of Christ?

How does your participation in prayer and the sacraments help you grow in faith as a witness to others?

How might you deepen your appreciation of the Church's liturgical life and your participation in the liturgy?

PRAYER

God our Father,
your Son taught his disciples to pray
and he left them the gift of his Body and Blood in the Eucharist,
to be celebrated in memory of him.
Through the Church's tradition,
the gifts of prayer, worship, and the sacraments are ours today.
Help us, in celebrating the liturgy, to mature in Christ,
and become ever more fully the place of his dwelling,
for the glory of his name, the sanctification of the world,
and our growth in holiness.
We ask this through Christ our Lord. Amen.

In the light of this reflection, is there anything else you would like to bring to the Lord in prayer?

RESTORING AND PROMOTING THE LITURGY

(SC 5 – 46)

UNDERSTANDING

Vatican II recalls the central saving truth of the Christian faith: that Jesus Christ, the Son of God, was born in human flesh, died on the cross, and rose again to new life. This is the work of our salvation, called the Paschal (or Easter) mystery. The Church's liturgy and sacraments make this work of salvation known and effective in our lives. The liturgy is a sacred action which draws us to the things of heaven. It is the 'pinnacle' to which all the Church's life ascends and the 'fountain' from which all the Church's life flows. Proper preparation, reverence, and dignity should characterise our celebration of the liturgy.

Vatican II wanted to reform the liturgy to enable greater participation and understanding by the people in the congregation. It addressed different aspects of liturgical celebration, promoting a dignified 'noble simplicity.' This included using the everyday language of the people, and giving greater prominence to readings from the Scriptures. The Council wanted to enhance the liturgical life of each diocese, and its parishes, especially through the celebration of Sunday Mass on the day of the Lord's Resurrection.

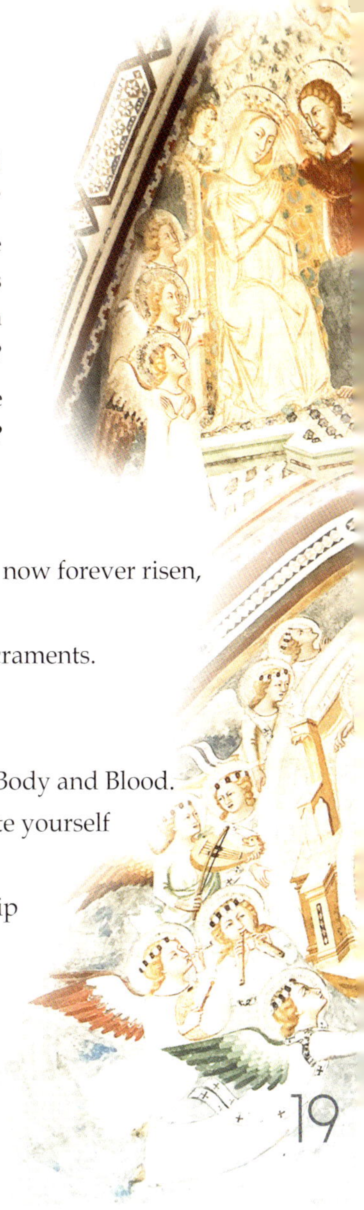

REFLECTION

How does the liturgy speak to you of the death and resurrection of the Lord Jesus?

How do you understand the liturgy to be the 'pinnacle' of the Christian life, towards which the whole of the Church's life is orientated; and also the 'fountain' from which all the Church's life flows?

How do the readings from the Scriptures, in the Liturgy of the Word, help your conversion, discipleship, and service?

PRAYER

Lord Jesus Christ, we believe that you died for us and are now forever risen,
and that you share with us the gift of eternal life.
You are present when we celebrate the liturgy and the sacraments.
You speak to us when the Scriptures are read.
You are with us in the Sacrifice of the Mass,
present in the priest and present supremely in your holy Body and Blood.
It is you who baptise, forgive, and heal; and you who unite yourself
to those who are confirmed, married, and ordained.
Help us to know and honour your presence in our worship
and to become, more clearly, your presence in our world.
Amen.

In the light of this reflection, is there anything else you would like to bring to the Lord in prayer?

THE MYSTERY OF THE HOLY EUCHARIST

(SC 47 – 58)

UNDERSTANDING

The Lord Jesus gave us the Holy Eucharist, the Mass, at the Last Supper the night before he died for us. The offering of his Body and Blood in the Mass, and the offering of his Body and Blood on the Cross, are one single Sacrifice for the salvation of the world. When we participate in the Mass we are not meant to be bystanders. Rather, we unite ourselves, devoutly and actively, to the Lord in his Word and in his Sacrament, gathered together as the Church.

Vatican II teaches that each part of the Mass should be clearly understood and related to the other parts of the celebration. This involved some changes and simplifications: using a wider selection of readings from the Bible; preaching on the Scriptures; including the Prayers of the Faithful; retaining some Latin for the parts of the Mass in common; distributing Holy Communion under both kinds - the Body of Christ and the Blood of Christ; priests concelebrating together around the altar. The Council asked that the Liturgy of the Word and the Liturgy of the Eucharist be celebrated in such a way that demonstrates their intimate connection as one single act of worship and praise. It refers to the two tables of the Mass - the table of God's Word and the table of the Lord's Body and Blood.

REFLECTION

What does it mean not to be a 'bystander' when you participate in the celebration of the Mass?

How do you understand the relationship between the different parts of the Mass?

What is your sense of the Liturgy of the Word and the Liturgy of the Eucharist – the two tables – as one single act of praise and worship?

PRAYER

Heavenly Father, we thank you that, in the Eucharist,
your Son gives us the very Body which he gave up for us
on the cross and the very Blood which he poured out
for the forgiveness of sins.
We ask you to give us a deeper love for the Mass.
May we participate more devoutly
and actively so that,
through both Word and Sacrament,
we might proclaim your Son's death,
and profess his Resurrection,
until he comes again.
We ask this through Christ our Lord.
Amen.

In the light of this reflection,
is there anything else
you would like to bring to the Lord in prayer?

THE SACRAMENTS AND SACRAMENTALS

(SC 59 – 82)

UNDERSTANDING

The Lord Jesus gave the Church the sacraments for our growth in holiness, to build up the Body of Christ, to teach us divine truths, and to help us worship. They are sacred outward signs of inward grace, where grace is the favour God grants freely so that we might share his life. The sacraments are effective. They bring about what they signal. They presuppose and strengthen our faith.

The seven sacraments of the Catholic Church are: Baptism; Confirmation; Eucharist; Penance and Reconciliation; Anointing of the Sick; Holy Orders; and Marriage. There are other signs called sacramentals, such as making the sign of the cross or sprinkling holy water. These point us towards the sacraments and help to sanctify our Christian living.

Vatican II proposed that the everyday language spoken by the people be used in celebrating the sacraments and sacramentals; that appropriate Rites (religious ceremonies) be prepared for different territories; and that the ancient stages of the adult catechumenate (the way for adults to be Baptised, Confirmed and receive the Eucharist) be restored. As a result, the Rites of Baptism, Confirmation, Penance, and Marriage were revised and the Anointing of the Sick was distinguished from the Rites for the Dying. The Funeral Liturgy was revised to express more clearly our Christian hope in the resurrection. In all these things, the Council's intention was to enable greater participation and understanding by the laity.

REFLECTION

Thinking about the seven sacraments, what aspect stands out for you as most significant in each celebration?

How do the sacraments and sacramentals help your personal discipleship and life of faith?

What might help you to deepen your understanding and appreciation of the sacraments and sacramentals?

PRAYER

Lord Jesus, thank you for the words and actions which accompanied your ministry on earth, and for giving us the sacraments to nourish
our Christian living and service.
Help us to be attentive to your presence
whenever we receive any of the sacraments.
May they be a source of holiness in the Church and in our lives,
and strengthen us to express our faith to the world.
Amen.

In the light of this reflection, is there anything else you would like to bring to the Lord in prayer?

PRAYING THE DIVINE OFFICE

(SC 83 – 101)

UNDERSTANDING

The Divine Office (sometimes called the Liturgy of the Hours, the Breviary, or the Prayer of the Church) is a pattern of prayer in the Church, across the day and night, through which time is sanctified by the praise of God. It provides texts of hymns, Scripture, and prayers that give a rhythm to each day, uniting our prayer through Christ to the Father in the Holy Spirit. The Psalms form a significant part of the prayer of the Church. These sacred texts would have been prayed by the Lord Jesus himself. The Divine Office is prayed at morning, during the day, in the evening and at night, by clergy, religious men and women, and lay people. Vatican II affirms the importance of the Divine Office in the Church, restoring the alignment of the prayers with set times of the day, such as at morning, evening and night prayer. In this way, prayer is spread throughout the day. There were some simplifications of the times and texts of prayers; a more generous inclusion of passages from Scripture and the writings of saints; and reforms for how religious communities pray the Office. The Council encourages, where possible, the Divine Office to be celebrated communally, by both clergy and laity, uniting the Church in the praise of God.

REFLECTION

Why do you think it is important for there to be a rhythm and pattern of prayer across the day in the life of the Church and each Christian?

Vatican II speaks of morning and evening prayer as the 'double hinge of the Divine Office.' What is your experience of praying in the morning and evening, whether with the Divine Office or other prayers?

What might lead to your own growth in prayer?

PRAYER

Heavenly Father,
your Son left us the pattern of prayer in his words and example.
We believe that you hear us when we lift our hearts and open our minds to you.
Help us to grow as people of prayer, to make time and space to come to you through your Son in the power of the Holy Spirit.
May we hear and listen. May we speak and be silent.
May we find you prayerfully in our daily rhythm of life so that your love and peace become ours.
We ask this through Christ our Lord.
Amen.

In the light of this reflection, is there anything else you would like to bring to the Lord in prayer?

THE LITURGICAL YEAR

(SC 102 – 111)

UNDERSTANDING

The heart of our faith is the death and resurrection of the Lord Jesus which we celebrate especially during Holy Week and at Easter. The liturgical year is the way in which the Church arranges the celebration of the great feasts of Christ and his Mother, of the saints, and of the different seasons around them. There is a yearly cycle to these feasts and seasons and their associated prayers and practices, all ordered around our salvation in Christ.

Vatican II reminds the Church of the importance of Christ's resurrection, celebrated at Easter, but also every Sunday, the Lord's Day. It is on Sunday that we gather together for the Eucharist to be renewed in faith and hope. The Council revised the liturgical year with a focus on the Paschal Mystery, but retained traditional feasts, seasons, and practices of piety and devotion. Central to this are the feasts of Christ our Saviour. Lent is renewed by a deeper appreciation of baptism and of being reconciled to God and to others. The commemoration of saints is commended, some for the universal Church, others for the local Church, as appropriate. The saints show how the holiness of Christ can be lived. They are examples for our imitation and support us by their prayers.

REFLECTION

What is your sense of the liturgical year and how do you keep the Church's feasts and seasons?

How do you make the connection between the Church's liturgical year and your own life of faith, for example during Lent and Advent?

Why do you think it is important to try and keep Sunday as a special day?

PRAYER

God our Father,
you created all time and seasons
to give shape and expression to our world and lives.
Our personal life of faith also has its own calendar
as we mark the feasts of your Son, of his Mother, of the liturgical seasons
and commemoration of the saints.
Help us to remember that all time belongs to you,
and that Christ, your Son, is the beginning and the end,
the Alpha and Omega of our existence.
May the liturgical year lead us more deeply into the mystery of Christ's
birth, life, death, resurrection, ascension and return in glory.
Like Our Lady and the Apostles, we pray for the descent of the
Holy Spirit to send us out in mission and service.
We ask this through Christ our Lord. Amen.

In the light of this reflection, is there anything else you would like to bring to the Lord in prayer?

SACRED MUSIC

(SC 112 – 121)

UNDERSTANDING

Vatican II affirms the ancient musical tradition of the Church in the liturgy; particularly as experienced through sacred chant. It encourages singing in the liturgy, both by clergy and laity. It teaches that a good musical tradition, drawing upon the Church's treasury, is to be maintained, with training and formation for musicians and choirs.

The Council affirms that Gregorian chant has a special and honoured place in the liturgy. This said, more popular religious music is also to be promoted, respecting the nature of the liturgical celebration and reflecting local customs. The organ has pride of place in Church music, but other instruments can also be used in accordance with the dignity and reverence required. Both musicians and composers have a special calling in the liturgical life of the Church. They are to use texts from the Scriptures and liturgical sources as the basis for their compositions.

REFLECTION

How do you think music and song enhance the Church's liturgical celebration?

It is often said that the person who sings in the liturgy actually prays twice. In what ways do you think song and music relate to prayer?

Do you have a favourite chant, hymn, or piece of religious music that speaks to you – what makes it special?

PRAYER

Lord Jesus,
we are an Easter people and Alleluia is our song.
We desire to lift our hearts, minds, and voices in music and song
to give praise, through you, to the Father,
in the strength of the Holy Spirit.
Teach us to be a people of praise
who can express, in music and song,
the desire within us to worship
in spirit and in truth.
Amen.

In the light of this reflection, is there anything else you would like to bring to the Lord in prayer?

SACRED ART AND FURNISHINGS

(SC 122 – 130)

UNDERSTANDING

Considering religious art and furnishings, Vatican II supports the work of making sacred objects and fittings that give praise and glory to God. Down the centuries, the Church has been a patron of the arts, always ensuring that sacred art and furnishings are appropriate for liturgical or spiritual use.

Vatican II recalls that the Church has never been tied to a particular artistic style or school. The test has always been, and remains, how any art or design gives glory to God. There is, therefore, encouragement for sacred art, buildings, vestments, vessels, and ornaments to be characterised by a noble beauty in the service of God and the liturgy. Sacred images for veneration are to be retained, although in proportionate numbers in any one place. The Church is to uphold the work of sacred artists, always ensuring that their art is fit for sacred purpose. The Church, too, is to educate future priests about the value and purpose of sacred art and furnishings.

REFLECTION

In what ways do you think sacred art and furnishings can turn hearts to God?

Is there a particular image, statue, or piece of art that speaks to you about an aspect of your faith?

Why do you think the Church has been a patron of fine art throughout history?

PRAYER

Heavenly Father, we are created in your image and likeness
to reflect your beauty and grandeur.
Give us eyes and hearts to appreciate beauty
as a sign of your presence in the world.
Help us to use sacred art and sacred objects
to come closer to you and the truths of our faith.
We ask this through Christ our Lord. Amen.

In the light of this reflection, is there anything else you would like to bring to the Lord in prayer?

AND I TELL YOU, YOU ARE PETER,
AND ON THIS ROCK I WILL BUILD MY CHURCH.

MT 16:18

PART 2

THE CHURCH

THE MYSTERY OF THE CHURCH

(LG 1 – 8)

UNDERSTANDING

Vatican II's *Dogmatic Constitution on the Church* was issued solemnly on 21 November 1964. It is referred to as *Lumen Gentium* (abbreviated as *LG)* which means *'the light of nations.'* This comes from the opening words in the original Latin text which translate as *'Christ is the Light of nations.'* The Council makes clear the Church's mission as the sacrament, the sacred sign, of our unity with God in Christ. The Church is part of God's plan to draw together, through the Holy Spirit, everyone who believes in Christ. The Church calls us to unity with Christ, and with each other, especially when we gather for the Eucharist. The Holy Spirit gives life to the Church and the hearts of the baptised. The Universal Church, present world-wide, shares the unity of the Father and the Son and the Holy Spirit. God guides the Church in truth and service, providing the gifts and fruits needed to proclaim the kingdom of Christ, something already present, but also still to be fulfilled. Vatican II offers different images for the Church taken from the Scriptures: God's flock or sheepfold; God's field or vineyard; God's building, household, or family; God's temple; the holy city, or new Jerusalem; the Jerusalem above; our Mother; the bride of Christ; Christ's body.

Christ is the head of his body the Church. All the baptised, each with different gifts and vocations, form the different parts of Christ's body, unified and animated by the Holy Spirit. Baptism unites us in sharing Christ's likeness. The Eucharist binds us together through the one bread and one cup. Christ has given the Church a visible 'framework' to fulfil the mission of proclaiming the Gospel. The Church is one, holy, catholic and apostolic, united under the successor of St Peter, the Pope, and the bishops in communion with him. As Christ was sent to announce the Good News of salvation, so the Church continues this work today, journeying through time, on pilgrimage, as the bearer of light and hope for the world.

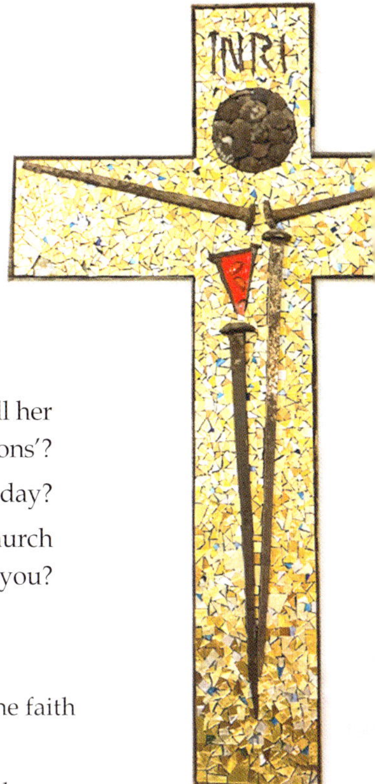

REFLECTION

What does it mean to you to say that the Church and all her members are called to be a 'light to the nations'?

In what ways do you experience the Church's mission today?

How do the different biblical images used for the Church speak to you?

PRAYER

God our Father, your Son founded the Church on the faith
of St Peter and the Apostles
to carry the light of your love and mercy to all peoples.
Throughout history your Church has witnessed to the Gospel,
announcing the death and resurrection of Christ as salvation for every person.
Unite your Church in faithfulness to Christ and in openness to the Holy Spirit.
We ask this through Christ our Lord. Amen.

In the light of this reflection, is there anything else you would like to bring to the Lord in prayer?

THE PEOPLE OF GOD

(LG 9 – 17)

UNDERSTANDING

Vatican II teaches that God's choice of the People of Israel foreshadows the new people who are born-again in Christ through water and the Holy Spirit. The Church gathers together into one, as the People of God, everyone who looks to Christ as their Saviour - laity, religious and clergy. Christ is the head of the Church and the source of her unity. He founded the Church as an instrument of salvation and he sends her out to preach the Gospel. The Church is presented in Scripture as the bride of Christ the bridegroom. The Church is also referred to in tradition as a mother. It is, therefore, common to speak of the Church using the pronouns she and her. St Peter describes those who are baptised into Christ as *'a chosen race, a royal priesthood, a holy nation.' (1 Pet 2:9)* All the baptised share in Christ's priesthood. This is related to, but distinct from, those who also share in Christ's priesthood through ordination. This ministerial priesthood is at the service of God's priestly people, offering on their behalf the Eucharistic sacrifice, the source and summit of the Christian life. In different ways, the sacraments unite the People of God to Christ as a priestly community in the Church. Every disciple, according to their vocation, is called to holiness of life.

The People of God also share in the prophetic office of Christ by giving witness to faith and charity. The Holy Spirit guides God's people in the truths of faith, under the Church's teaching authority. Holiness grows through living the virtues, and through the spiritual graces as God assigns them. As members of the kingdom of

Christ, the People of God is spread universally across the world, diverse in gifts and functions, but united in the Church under the Pope. Christ offers salvation in the Catholic Church which always seeks dialogue and unity with other Christians and non-Christians. The Church remains faithful to her missionary nature and purpose: to make disciples, baptise, teach, and preach the Good News.

REFLECTION

What does it mean to you, through your baptism, to have a share in Christ's priesthood?

How does participation in the Eucharistic celebration strengthen your faith?

How might you share in the Church's mission to promote unity?

PRAYER

Almighty Father, in Christ we are a priestly people,
called to holiness, witness, and service.
May we use the talents and graces you give us
for the mission of your Church,
to grow in holiness and faith, to build up the People of God,
and to reach out to those who do not know, or ignore, your Son.
We ask this through Christ our Lord. Amen.

In the light of this reflection, is there anything else you would like to bring to the Lord in prayer?

THE CHURCH'S STRUCTURE AND THE OFFICE OF BISHOP

(LG 18 – 29)

UNDERSTANDING

Vatican II reiterates previous teaching which affirms that Christ established different ministries in the Church to serve the growth and holiness of the People of God. The Lord Jesus appointed St Peter and the apostles, with the Popes and the bishops respectively as their successors, to exercise the ministry of shepherding and teaching, inspired by the Holy Spirit. The apostles fulfilled the evangelising mission given them by the Lord. To assist this they, and their successors, appointed others - priests and deacons - to share the responsibility of leadership, preaching, and pastoral care. This threefold pattern of ministry – bishops, priests, and deacons - is willed by Christ for the life of the Church and the service of the Gospel.

St Peter and the apostles formed an 'apostolic college,' which their successors, the Pope and the bishops, continue today. The bishops must always act collegially, within this college, united to the Pope as its head. The Pope, as successor of St Peter, is the principle of unity for the Church, for her bishops and her faithful. Individual bishops exercise care over a particular part of the Church which is the portion of the People of God entrusted to them, always mindful of the Church's unity as a whole. The bishops receive the same mission Christ gave to the apostles and are aided by the Holy Spirit. They are to preach and teach the Catholic faith authentically, and, along with the Pope, should receive allegiance from the faithful. In certain circumstances, the Pope, or the Pope with the college of bishops, can affirm the Church's faith infallibly, that is, without error, to safeguard the Truths of belief. Bishops are to oversee the local Church, working with priests and deacons, to enable the sacramental life of faith to flourish in service of the whole People of God.

REFLECTION

How do you think the three-fold ministry of bishops, priests and deacons serves the Church's ministry?

What is your experience of working collaboratively in the Church's mission?

How do you understand the role of the Pope in relation to the Church?

PRAYER

Lord Jesus, you willed that your Church
should be built on apostolic foundations.
You gave to St Peter and the apostles
the authority to guide your Church,
and to keep it faithful to the truth.
Grant strength and wisdom to our Holy Father, to our bishops, priests, and deacons.
May they serve as good shepherds after your own heart,
to lead your people in faithfulness, nourished by the sacraments,
and united always more closely to you. Amen.

In the light of this reflection, is there anything else you would like to bring to the Lord in prayer?

THE LAITY

(LG 30 - 38)

UNDERSTANDING

Vatican II teaches that everything that is said of the People of God applies equally to lay people, religious, and clergy. There are, however, some aspects that are particular to the laity. The Church's mission to announce salvation requires the cooperation of all the People of God, each according to their vocation. Lay people share Christ's life by baptism, participating in his priestly, prophetic, and kingly offices. The laity are not clergy or religious. They have the specific vocation to make Christ present in the secular world through their witness of faith, hope, and charity. All the People of God share in the same dignity granted by baptism and, without exception, are called to holiness of life. The Church's pastors and lay faithful are to collaborate in the service of each other for sake of the proclamation of the Gospel. The unique calling of lay people is to be present in the world like 'yeast in the dough' (see Mt 13:33) - in business and secular life, in culture, and in marriage, family, and home life - furthering the saving work of Christ.

The mission of lay people draws its life from the graces of baptism and confirmation, and from the Eucharist, prayer, and apostolic service. The laity are witnesses to hope, called to evangelise though faithfulness to Christ in daily life. They show forth the spirit of Christ in serving the Lord's kingdom in the world. Both pastors and lay people have rights and responsibilities in the Church, working together with mutual

respect to testify to the hope Christ's resurrection offers. Lay people are signs of Christ's presence to bring the Gospel to life in the world.

REFLECTION

How would you describe your vocation to live out your baptismal calling?

What do you think are some of the specific ways in which lay people can evangelise?

How might you be called to grow in holiness of life and witness to Christ?

PRAYER

Holy Spirit, come and renew us; send us new life as you did at Pentecost.
Ignite the flame of faith in our hearts.
Give us words so we can share our faith with gentleness and confidence.
We ask you, Holy Spirit, to enable all the lay faithful of Christ's Church
to fulfil their baptismal vocation as evangelists and missionaries in the world.
Give new gifts and graces so that the Gospel might reach all peoples and places.
Grant unity to the Church, that each member might fulfil
their vocation by working collaboratively for the
spread of the Gospel and the sanctification of the world.
Come, Holy Spirit. Amen.

In the light of this reflection, is there anything else you would like to bring to the Lord in prayer?

THE UNIVERSAL CALL TO HOLINESS

(LG 39 – 42)

UNDERSTANDING

The Church is the bride of Christ for whom he gave up his life, to make her holy. The Church's holiness comes from Christ. Vatican II confirms that everyone in the Church shares the same call to holiness, although expressed in different ways. Every baptised disciple is called to the perfection of charity. The Lord Jesus calls us to be perfect as our heavenly Father is perfect (Mt 5:48) and sent the Holy Spirit to increase within our hearts our love for God and for our neighbour. In Christ we are made holy, a gift to be treasured and nurtured. We follow in Christ's footsteps, seeking to live like him, giving glory to God and service to others. This example is set before us in the lives of countless saints down the ages.

The path of holiness involves each person making their own particular journey, in Christ, to the Father, through the Holy Spirit. Bishops, priests, and deacons must fulfil their vocation to holiness through the faithful exercise of the ministry entrusted to them. Similarly, those who are married, parents, widowed, or single are all called to find holiness in the situations in which they live, as are those who face challenges and suffering. Faith in Christ strengthens us for whatever life brings as we find and do God's will. Holiness involves sacrifice and virtue. For some, this means following Christ by giving witness as a martyr. For others, it means total dedication to Christ. For every disciple, however, the way of holiness enables a life of loving devotion and service for the sake of God's kingdom. At the heart of holiness is the practice of love towards God and others, nourished by the spiritual life and the sacraments, especially the Eucharist.

REFLECTION

What does the call to holiness mean to you and your life of discipleship?

What are the challenges you face in living a holy life, and how might they be overcome?

Which saints speak to you about how to live the call to holiness of life?

PRAYER

Almighty Father, your Son offers the example of perfection in obedience to your will.
He called us to be perfect as you, heavenly Father, are perfect.
We ask for the strengthening of the Holy Spirit
so that, according to our own vocation,
we can grow in holiness and seek the perfection of charity.
Help us not to be discouraged by our failures,
but to trust in your love, shown in the Lord Jesus,
so that we might always journey in hope as we try to love faithfully and generously.
We ask this through Christ our Lord. Amen.

In the light of this reflection, is there anything else you would like to bring to the Lord in prayer?

RELIGIOUS WOMEN AND MEN

(LG 43 – 47)

UNDERSTANDING

There are many different ways of living religious life, or a specially dedicated, or consecrated, life in the Church. These all focus around the evangelical counsels of poverty, chastity, and obedience. Each congregation of religious women (sisters or nuns) and religious men (monks, friars, priests or brothers) lives according to a rule of life, either in a monastery, convent, priory or friary, or a community exercising apostolic and missionary service. Vatican II reminds religious they are called to holiness through joyful lives of witness and charity. A vocation to religious life grows from baptism. It is an act of consecration to service in the Church through solemn vows and promises. By their life-long commitment, religious and consecrated men and women are signs of the presence of the kingdom of God among us.

Religious life is subject to the authority and discernment of the Church, especially when new associations or congregations are established. Female and male religious model themselves on Christ in their desire to give themselves totally to God. In response to God's call, they freely choose to live in poverty, chastity, and obedience, so that they might be rich, loving, and free, making a gift of their lives to the Father, through Christ, in the power of the Holy Spirit.

REFLECTION

Why do you think God calls people to religious and consecrated life?

What do you think is the important witness and service religious and consecrated men and women give to the Church and in the world?

How do you think the choice to live in poverty, chastity, and obedience is a sign of God's kingdom?

PRAYER

Lord Jesus,
you call certain women and men to live a radical pathway of discipleship.
They are to be rich through poverty, loving through chastity,
and free through obedience.
Their lives give witness to the enduring truths of your kingdom
as they choose to serve the Church and the world in holiness.
Give strength to all who are called to religious life.
May they be signs of the joy and love
which come from total dedication to following you,
the way, the truth, and the life. Amen.

In the light of this reflection, is there anything else you would like to bring to the Lord in prayer?

THE PILGRIM CHURCH

(LG 48 – 51)

UNDERSTANDING

The Church is on a pilgrimage through time towards eternity. This journey will be completed when the Church and her members reach the glory of heaven and all things are united in Christ. Vatican II speaks of the 'eschatological nature of the pilgrim Church.' The word eschatological (from the Greek word for 'last') means that which comes at the end. The Church was established by Christ with a final destination in heaven. As the sign of salvation for the world, the Church draws people towards eternal life when her pilgrimage, and that of her members, will be complete and fulfilled. Until then, the Church, marked with a genuine, but imperfect holiness, continues to announce the Good News of Christ. By her sacramental life, the Church anticipates the glorious future promised her by the Lord.

The possibility of heaven comes to us because of the death and resurrection of Christ. Each disciple lives in the hope of being united with Christ in the heavenly Church. Vatican II affirms that the 'Mystical Body of Christ,' the Church on earth, exists in relationship with those who have gone before us, especially Our Blessed Lady and the saints. Those who have followed Christ faithfully chart the way for us to follow so that we might also come to share the life of glory. We are in fellowship with the saints in heaven and also with each other as pilgrims in the Church on earth. We ask the prayers of those in heaven. The liturgy, especially the Eucharist, offers a foretaste of the heavenly banquet. We offer our own prayers for those who have died and who are making their journey to eternal life. The vocation of the Church is to seek union with the most Holy Trinity, that we might praise forever the Father, the Son, and the Holy Spirit.

REFLECTION

In what ways are you on a journey as a disciple of the Lord Jesus in his Church and in the world?

What do you think it means for the Church to be on pilgrimage towards union with Christ in heaven?

In what ways might you grow in friendship and fellowship with the saints and with others?

PRAYER

Almighty Father,
by his death and resurrection your Son has opened up the way to eternal life.
As we make our journey of faith, as pilgrims in your pilgrim Church,
teach us the ways of holiness so that, always growing in love,
we might live on earth with our hearts set on the things of heaven.
May we look to Our Lady and the saints to guide us to eternity.
We ask this through Christ our Lord. Amen.

In the light of this reflection, is there anything else you would like to bring to the Lord in prayer?

THE BLESSED VIRGIN MARY AND THE CHURCH

(LG 52 – 69)

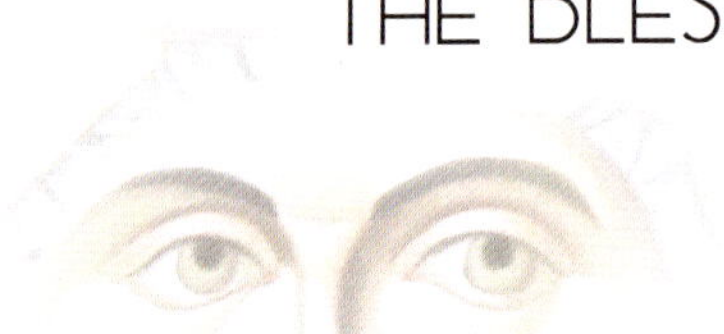

UNDERSTANDING

In the final chapter of *Lumen Gentium*, the bishops at Vatican II turned their attention to the Blessed Virgin Mary, the Mother of our Saviour Jesus Christ, true God and true man. Mary is honoured with the ancient title of Mother of God. She has a unique role in God's plan to send his Son to redeem the world. She is the supreme example of what it means to be a disciple, to be faithful and attentive to God's promises. She is a model for imitation by every Christian. Mary cooperated with God's will in the most beautiful way. Her obedient 'yes' to God's invitation brought the Lord Jesus to birth. Throughout her life, during her pregnancy, Christ's birth, infancy, hidden life, and public ministry, the Virgin Mary made her pilgrimage of faith with him. At the end of her life, she was assumed, body and soul, into heaven to reign as Queen of the saints and to guide the Church by her maternal intercession.

Jesus Christ is the sole mediator between God and humanity. All the Blessed Virgin Mary is, and does, comes from the merits of Christ. She is bound intimately to his work of salvation as the Mother of the Church. She is the first and perfect disciple, whose prayer sustains the Church's pilgrimage of faith. For this reason, Our Lady has a special place in the Church's worship and devotion. She is honoured as the living Mother of God in heaven, she whom we look to for spiritual comfort, encouragement, and help. From the Scriptures and the tradition of the Church, Our Lady is a sign of hope for the People of God and for the whole world.

REFLECTION

Why do you think the Church gives such honour to the Blessed Virgin Mary?

How would you describe your relationship with Our Lady and her relationship with the Church?

What prayers and devotions, or sites of pilgrimage, connected to Our Lady have been helpful to you?

PRAYER

O Blessed Virgin Mary,
Mother of our Lord and God, Jesus Christ,
and Mother of God's pilgrim people in the Church,
we look to you and thank God for your willingness
to bring the Lord Jesus to birth, conceived by the Holy Spirit.
Thank you for your maternal care for Our Lord,
and your motherly tenderness towards us, his disciples.
Please pray for us that we might have faith like yours,
that we might do what your Son tells us,
that we might stand with him in our suffering
and rise with him in his glory. Amen.

In the light of this reflection, is there anything else you would like to bring to the Lord in prayer?

LONG AGO, AT MANY TIMES AND IN MANY WAYS, GOD SPOKE TO OUR FATHERS BY THE PROPHETS, BUT IN THESE DAYS HE HAS SPOKEN TO US BY HIS SON.

HEB 1:1-2

PART 3

DIVINE REVELATION

GOD'S REVELATION

(DV 1 – 6)

UNDERSTANDING

Vatican II's *Dogmatic Constitution on Divine Revelation* was issued solemnly on 18 November 1965. It is often referred to as *Dei Verbum,* abbreviated as *DV*. This is Latin for *'word of God'* and comes from the Constitution's opening sentence in the original Latin text which translates as *'Hearing the word of God…'* Standing in continuity with the teaching of previous Church Councils, Vatican II confirms that God has shown himself to the world (through revelation) and that what has been revealed has been handed on throughout history (by transmission). This is so that all generations might receive the message of salvation; so that we, and our world, might believe, hope, and love.

God has revealed himself through his Son, Jesus Christ, the Word made flesh, that we might enter into divine friendship. From the beginning of creation, and through the People of Israel, God has unveiled a divine plan where words and actions have revealed divine truth. This plan of salvation was fulfilled through the Eternal Word, the second person of the Holy Trinity, who became flesh in the Lord Jesus. His birth, life, ministry, passion, death, resurrection and ascension confirmed God's revelation of the promise of reconciliation and everlasting life.

We respond to God's revelation through the obedience of faith. Natural human reason can lead us to a knowledge of God. It is, however, God's grace, his free and undeserved help, which assists our response in faith, supported by the gifts of the Holy Spirit. Divine revelation is God's communication of himself to the world so that we might know and share his life.

REFLECTION

How would you explain to someone why God chose to reveal himself to us?

What has been your experience of believing for yourself what God has revealed?

How do you think human reasoning might help people to believe, and what difference does faith make?

PRAYER

God our loving Father,
thank you for creating our world and the human race.
Thank you for speaking to us
through people and events across the history of salvation.
Thank you for sending your Son, the Lord Jesus,
to show us your love in our human flesh.
Help us to be open to your word of life,
and to receive in our hearts and minds the gift of your divine truth.
We ask this through Christ our Lord. Amen.

In the light of this reflection, is there anything else you would like to bring to the Lord in prayer?

HANDING ON DIVINE REVELATION

(DV 7 – 10)

UNDERSTANDING

Christ commanded the apostles to preach the Gospel of salvation to the ends of the earth. They handed on faithfully to others what they themselves had received from the Lord. They did this, first of all, through the spoken word and then through written texts. This work of passing on what God has revealed, supremely so in Christ, was entrusted, through the apostles, to their successors, the bishops. Sacred Tradition (that which has been handed on) and sacred Scripture (that which is written down in both the Old and New Testaments) form a 'mirror' where God can be seen and contemplated. Assisted by the Holy Spirit, whether by word of mouth, or in writing, the apostles transmitted to their successors all that was necessary for growth in holiness and faith. This continues today. God speaks through Tradition and Scripture which form a single deposit of the word of God given to the Church.

Vatican II teaches that the responsibility for authentically interpreting the word of God rests with the Church's magisterium, her living teaching authority. The word magisterium comes from the Latin word *magister* which means master or teacher. The magisterium's role is to safeguard the faith entrusted to the

Church by the Lord and contained in sacred Tradition and sacred Scripture. These three – Tradition, Scripture and magisterium – always belong together, so the truth and unity of faith can be preserved.

REFLECTION

Why do you think it is important to pass on the truths of our faith authentically?

In what ways, in your life, has the faith been handed on to you?

How can you hand on the faith to others; what are some of the challenges and opportunities in doing this?

PRAYER

Lord Jesus, you preached the Good News of the kingdom
in your words and in your actions,
and especially by your death and resurrection.
You asked your apostles to take what you had revealed to them
to the ends of the world, baptising and teaching all nations.
Your apostles then appointed successors, the bishops, to continue this
work in your name, for your glory and the salvation of your people.
May the word of God, entrusted to your Church,
in sacred Tradition and sacred Scripture,
always be our living word of life, hope, and joy. Amen.

In the light of this reflection, is there anything else you would like to bring to the Lord in prayer?

THE DIVINE INSPIRATION AND INTERPRETATION OF SCRIPTURE

(DV 11 – 13)

UNDERSTANDING

Vatican II teaches that the truths necessary for our salvation are contained in sacred Scripture. They were written down by human authors who were prompted and inspired by the Holy Spirit. It was in the fourth century that the Church, through the Pope acting with the bishops, brought together authoritatively the sacred writings of the Old and New Testaments to form what we know as the Christian Bible. The list of books included is sometimes called the canon of Scripture and was approved by the Church. God inspired human authors and teachers to compile the Scriptures, through which God speaks to all peoples in all ages.

We gain more understanding of the Scriptures when we appreciate the context in which the divinely inspired human authors lived and wrote. The Bible contains differing types of literature, from different cultures, written by different people at different times. We need to take this on board when reading the Scriptures. The Council encourages us to see each part of Scripture in the context of the whole Bible, and of the Tradition, and interpret it subject to the Church's magisterium.

Scripture reveals that God has made known to us his eternal wisdom for our well-being and salvation. Divine truths are spoken through human language so that we might be drawn to the things of heaven.

REFLECTION

How would you explain how God speaks through the Scriptures?

Are any particular passages of Scripture important to you because of how God has spoken to you through them?

In what ways could you be more open to the Lord speaking through the Scriptures?

PRAYER

Almighty Father,
since time began you have loved the world.
You called the People of Israel to receive your truth.
At the appointed time, you sent your Son
to show us your love and bring us to you.
May the words and works of salvation, recorded in the Scriptures,
be alive for us today in your Church.
Help us to be hearers of your word, receivers of your word,
doers of your word, and sharers of your word.
We ask this through Christ our Lord. Amen.

In the light of this reflection, is there anything else you would like to bring to the Lord in prayer?

THE OLD TESTAMENT

(DV 14 – 16)

UNDERSTANDING

Christians refer to the parts of the Bible written before the birth of Christ as the Old Testament. The word *testament* is related to the word *testify* and carries with it the sense of the account of a witness. The Old Testament is the witness of God's actions and words towards the People of Israel. With them God entered into *covenant* – the word for a special relationship between God and his people where both parties promise fidelity. *'You will be my people,'* God says to the People of Israel, *'and I will be your God.'* (See: Gen 17:7; Ez 36:28)

Choosing leaders such as Abraham and Moses, God revealed himself to the Israelites. He spoke through kings and prophets throughout their history. This prepared the way for Christ to come as redeemer through a New Covenant, a new relationship, established by his death and resurrection. Vatican II recalls the great theologian, St Augustine, who said that God, who is the inspiration and divine author of Scripture, arranged for the message of the New Testament to be concealed in the Old, and the message of the Old Testament to be shown forth in the New.

The books, or writings, of the Old Testament are an integral part of the message of salvation.

REFLECTION

What important witness about God's faithfulness do you think is shown in the Old Testament?

What do you think it means for God to make a special relationship with the People of Israel?

In what ways do you think the message of the New Testament is concealed in the Old Testament and the message of the Old Testament is revealed in the New Testament?

PRAYER

Almighty God,
giver of all good things,
you have shown yourself to us through creation
and through your closeness to your people.
Through the patriarchs and prophets,
may we receive the truth and wisdom of your promises.
With the people you first made your own
may we attain thc fullness of redemption.
Through Christ our Lord. Amen.

In the light of this reflection, is there anything else you would like to bring to the Lord in prayer?

THE NEW TESTAMENT

(DV 17 – 20)

UNDERSTANDING

The New Testament records the coming of Christ together with all that followed in his life, ministry, death, resurrection, and ascension. Added to this are Pentecost and the experiences and writings of the early Church, especially those of St Paul and the apostles. The New Testament is the word of God sourced in the living Lord, Jesus Christ, God's Son. When the Lord ascended to his Father and promised to send the Holy Spirit upon the Church, the mission was set in motion to share the Good News of salvation. The apostles were sent out to proclaim new life and hope in Christ.

Vatican II emphasises that the Gospels have a unique place in the Scriptures as the accounts of the life and teaching of our Saviour. The Church believes the four Gospels of Matthew, Mark, Luke, and John communicate accurately and faithfully the truth about Christ and his mission. This truth was first transmitted by the apostles through the spoken word and then committed to writing so there would be a permanent record of what Christ did and taught. The Gospels are eyewitness accounts from the apostles and their contemporaries, shared honestly and committed to text. The other writings in the New Testament are gathered with the Gospels to preserve the fullness of faith from the early Church, under the guidance of the Holy Spirit who unites us in the truth.

REFLECTION

What place do the Gospels have in your life as a disciple?

What passage from the New Testament speaks to you most powerfully about the new life and hope you have in Christ?

How might the Scriptures have a better and wider place in your personal journey of faith and in the communal journey of Christians together?

PRAYER

Lord Jesus Christ,
word of God and word of life:
You speak to us yourself through your Holy Gospel.
You are alive in your word through the Holy Spirit.
When the Gospel is proclaimed, you are made present.
When the Gospel is received, you make your home within us.
Give us ears and hearts and minds and lips of faith.
Given us hands and feet of service.
Let your Gospel be our life;
and let our life be your Gospel. Amen.

In the light of this reflection, is there anything else you would like to bring to the Lord in prayer?

SACRED SCRIPTURE IN THE LIFE OF THE CHURCH

(DV 21 – 26)

UNDERSTANDING

The Church honours the sacred Scriptures which, together with sacred Tradition, form the supreme basis of our faith. We are fed and nourished by the Scriptures, especially in the liturgy and through sermons rooted in God's word.

Vatican II teaches that the Scriptures should be accessible to lay people. Respecting the original languages of the Scriptures, and the first translations into Latin, the Church also seeks to provide accurate versions of the Bible in everyday language, with explanatory notes. Opening the treasure of the Scriptures helps to deepen an understanding of this living word at all levels. Under the guidance of the Church, and faithful to Tradition, the study of Scripture is to be promoted.

Sacred Scripture contains the divinely inspired word of God. It is the foundation or 'soul' of theology, and the basis for preaching within the liturgy, for catechesis, and for instruction in the faith. Both clergy and catechists should be imbued with God's word. The Council recalls St Jerome's affirmation that *'ignorance of Scripture is ignorance of Christ.'* Prayerfully reading the Scriptures allows God to speak to us so that we might hear his holy word and put it into practice.

REFLECTION

How do you understand the complementarity between being fed by Christ in the Scriptures and being fed by Christ in the Eucharist?

What do you think are some of the obstacles to reading and praying with Scripture, and how might these be overcome?

How might you be more prayerfully attentive to the Lord speaking through his word?

PRAYER

Heavenly Father,
thank you for giving us the Scriptures
through your Church,
under the direction and inspiration of the Holy Spirit.
Help us to know we are people of your word,
the living word and person of Jesus Christ.
Guide us to hear him speaking through the Scriptures,
revealing your love for everyone Lord. Amen.

In the light of this reflection, is there anything else you would like to bring to the Lord in prayer?

GO INTO ALL THE WORLD AND PROCLAIM THE GOSPEL
TO THE WHOLE CREATION.

MK 16:15

PART 4

THE CHURCH IN THE MODERN WORLD

HUMANITY AND THE MODERN WORLD

(GS 1 – 10)

UNDERSTANDING

Vatican II's *Pastoral Constitution on the Church in the Modern World* was issued solemnly on 7 December 1965. It is referred to as *Gaudium et Spes*, abbreviated as GS, the Latin words for *'joys and hopes,'* which comes from the opening sentence of the original Latin text which translates: *'The joys and the hopes, the griefs and the anxieties of the people of this age, especially those who are poor or in any way afflicted, these are the joys and hopes, the griefs and anxieties of the followers of Christ.'* Vatican II wanted to address some of the important concerns of humanity and our world which are also concerns for the Church. World history, and present-day reality, paint a picture of successes and failures regarding reverence for the human person, human dignity, and creation. The Gospel offers a message of transformation to all peoples, and for all times. The Church has received the mission from Christ to witness to this truth.

Vatican II calls upon the Church to *'read the signs of the times,'* to take stock of our world in the light of Gospel. Amidst so many changes, there are important truths which must not be lost. Even in a world of progress, inequality and injustice remain. Many people live between hope and anxiety. Science and technology provide blessings to humanity, but can also be controlling and destructive. The gap between rich and poor, in all senses, and at all levels, creates a disconnection that undermines goods and values which are essential for human flourishing, including religion. Transition can increase strains and tensions in relationships. In different ways, humanity experiences a quest for control which can sometimes compromise the deeper needs of human worth and living. Announcing Christ as Saviour, Vatican II presents his Gospel as the answer to humanity's struggle with sin and the search for meaning. It sheds light on the problems of our day.

REFLECTION

Looking at our world today, and reading 'the signs of our times', what do you see as humanity's joys and hopes, griefs and anxieties?

What is your sense of the inequalities between people today?

How would you describe the hope that Christ and his Gospel offers?

PRAYER

God our Heavenly Father,
you loved our world so much that you sent your only Son,
not to condemn our world, but so that, through him,
our world might be saved.
Help us to read the signs of our times
in the light of his Gospel of love, truth, and justice.
We raise up to you the joys, hopes, sorrows and concerns of
our world and all its nations and peoples.
Bless and sustain us in the ways of peace and reconciliation,
of integrity and solidarity.
We ask this through Christ our Lord. Amen.

In the light of this reflection, is there anything else you would like to bring to the Lord in prayer?

THE CALL AND DIGNITY OF THE HUMAN PERSON

(GS 11 – 22)

UNDERSTANDING

In the light of faith, Vatican II states that the Church's mission to the world, shared by the whole People of God, is to promote and defend all that is authentically human. The human person is central, created in the image of God and given stewardship over the earth. God created man and woman for relationship, as social beings, to live within the gift of freedom before God and each other. Both the Scriptures and human experience teach that this original harmony is damaged by the selfishness of sin which makes human beings turn inwards, away from God and from others. There is a struggle between good and evil, between light and darkness. But, within the human heart, the knowledge of God and of truth can be found. This is expressed through the practical judgement of conscience, which does not discover the truth, but applies the truth. Even given the complexities of life, the search for truth draws us towards what God has revealed as good.

The resurrection of the Lord Jesus means Christians live with hope. Some people cannot believe because they have rejected God, others because they have never properly sought or found God. While taking the effects of atheism seriously, the Church calls her members to announce, witness, and teach faithfully the Gospel of Christ. We make sense of our humanity through the Lord

Jesus who took our flesh so we might share his life. Disciples, and all people of good will, are strengthened by genuine hope which, in Christ, becomes life in abundance.

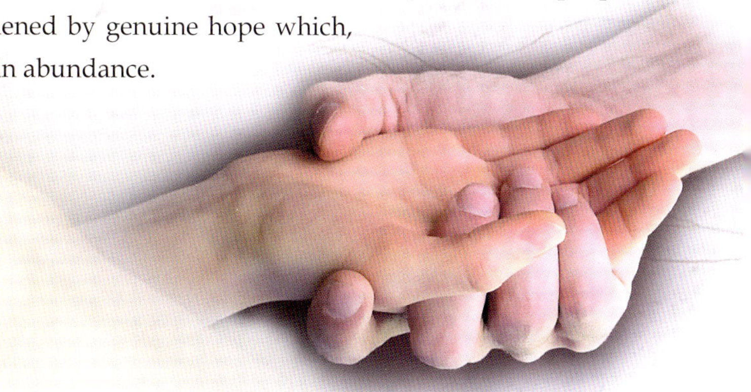

REFLECTION

What does it mean to you to be created in God's image?

How do you experience the effects of sin?

How would you explain your faith in God to someone who does not believe, and how would you share with them the hope you have that comes from Christ?

PRAYER

Lord Jesus, you destroyed our death by dying on the cross;
you restored our life by rising from the dead;
you offer us forgiveness and healing, and have opened up the way to eternal life.
Help us to see and love and serve every person, and our world,
with your eyes, your heart, and your hands.
May we witness today that you are alive,
that you offer meaning and purpose to human existence, in joy and freedom. Amen.

In the light of this reflection, is there anything else you would like to bring to the Lord in prayer?

HUMAN COMMUNITY

(GS 23 – 32)

UNDERSTANDING

Vatican II reminds us that human beings need each other. We form a human community, a communion, which seeks to deepen the spiritual and moral character given to us by our Creator. God desires that human beings live as a family. Each person is created in God's image and invited to embrace the commandment to love God and their neighbour, seeking fulfilment through self-giving. Our social life together should enhance our common humanity and protect fundamental human rights and responsibilities. We are interdependent. We need each other, personally, socially, nationally, and internationally, not least in working to ensure everyone has access to the basic freedoms and necessities of life. Our social life should be ordered to the good of each person and of our life together.

Vatican II asserts the dignity of each person without exception, and the need to care for those suffering or threatened, whether in the womb, during life, or at the end of life. Any disregard for the sanctity of life or for justice must be opposed. Charity, friendship, and mercy underpin our common life, always served by truth. There is no place for inequality or discrimination where human rights are concerned. Working for the common good of all people means that both our public and private institutions should create a climate of human friendship and solidarity. In this, we are to reflect the life and example of Christ and the message of his Gospel.

REFLECTION

What does it mean to you to speak of the world as a human family?

How do you think we are interdependent on each other, individually, socially, and internationally?

How do you think the Church can promote the common good and combat injustice?

PRAYER

Almighty Father,
you have created us in your image
and called us to new life in Christ your Son.
Help us to contribute to building up the common good,
so that human life and dignity might be secured for all.
May our service of others honour the harmony and peace
you desire for all peoples.
We ask this through Christ our Lord. Amen.

In the light of this reflection, is there anything else you would like to bring to the Lord in prayer?

HUMAN ACTIVITY IN THE WORLD

(GS 33 – 39)

UNDERSTANDING

Vatican II recognises that people today often look to science, technology, commerce and industry, or simply human self-sufficiency, rather than things of faith. This raises important questions about human activity and its relationship with the truths of faith which must always be safeguarded by the Church. Human progress has brought many benefits which can be seen as gifts of God. The Church is not opposed to human endeavours, but always situates them within what God has revealed, not least about the human person and human dignity.

Teaching about autonomy – the right to make decisions – Vatican II cautions against human action being separated from the essential values of the human person and the world as God's creation. For the Church, genuine human development cannot exclude God or religious faith. Even when situations in the world are marked by self-interest, we retain a fundamental hope in the power of Christ's cross and resurrection. The world is transformed by love. This is shown in the life of the Lord Jesus. It is activated in human hearts by the gifts of the Holy Spirit. Our world is scarred by sin, but all things can and will be restored in Christ. The kingdom of God, already present in mystery, will be brought to completion.

REFLECTION

What do you think is the fundamental message about the human person which the Church offers to the world today?

In a world of science and atheism, why do you think faith in Christ remains important?

What signs do you think indicate that the kingdom of God is already present in our world, albeit in an incomplete way?

PRAYER

Holy Spirit,
you descended at Pentecost and brought unity to the Church.
Come with gifts of unity, peace, and wisdom for our world.
Help us to value people and to use things,
and never to use people and value things.
Come, Spirit of light and hope,
do not let the power of sin compromise the dignity of human life.
Breathe into us a respect for creation so that all progress and development
is a reflection of the truth that our world and each person is divinely created.
Come, Holy Spirit. Amen.

In the light of this reflection, is there anything else you would like to bring to the Lord in prayer?

THE CHURCH'S ROLE IN THE WORLD TODAY

(GS 40 – 45)

UNDERSTANDING

The Church makes known the meaning of human existence in relation to God's plan of salvation. Human beings can know themselves better through following Christ and living according to his Gospel. The Church's mission is religious and spiritual, empowered by faith and charity in the service of all, especially those most in need. The Church is no threat to whatever is truly good in our world.

Enlivened by the Gospel, Christians take their place in the world. Their feet and hands are on earth, while their eyes and heart look to heaven. For disciples, faith and life cannot be separated. We must fulfil our obligations to others and the common good. In this, the laity make a specific contribution by sowing the seeds of faith in secular life. Together in the Church, and all inspired by the Holy Spirit, clergy, religious and laity, are beacons of spiritual and human goods. Reading the signs of the times, in the light of Christ's teaching, the Church adapts to each age so the Gospel can be proclaimed faithfully. Always on pilgrimage, until the end of time, the Church is the sacrament, the sign of salvation for all people, showing God's love until the Lord comes again.

REFLECTION

While carrying out a mission on earth, how does the Church also point you towards heaven?

What do you think it means to be a beacon of human and spiritual goods?

How might the whole Church – clergy, religious and laity – preach the Gospel in changing times? How might you take up your part in this?

PRAYER

Almighty Father,
your Son founded the Church to be the sacrament of salvation in the world
until he comes again.
We believe that the Church, and every disciple, is in the world,
but not of the world.
Help us to have a spiritual outlook, to seek all things,
in the Church and in the world,
through the lens of faith and hope in your Son.
We ask this through Christ our Lord.
Amen.

In the light of this reflection, is there anything else you would like to bring to the Lord in prayer?

PROMOTING THE DIGNITY OF MARRIAGE AND FAMILY LIFE

(GS 46 – 52)

UNDERSTANDING

For Vatican II, the well-being of individuals, society, and the Church, is intimately connected with the well-being of marriage and family life. While there are challenges to marriage and family in the world, the Church supports the natural dignity of marriage which, in Christ, is raised to a sacrament. Marriage and family form a community of love, established by God, where a man and woman enter into a mutually enriching and self-giving permanent relationship, for the good of each other and of their children and society. The love between husband and wife is blessed by Christ and their union reflects the unbreakable union between Christ and his Church. Spouses are bound together by their free, faithful, and fruitful gift of themselves to each other for their growth in love and holiness. As fathers and mothers they are to welcome the children God may send them, creating families which lovingly nurture the life of faith in the home. Husband and wife share in God's creative love when they bring new life into the world.

Despite obstacles to married life, to the raising of children, and to the flourishing of the family, the Church holds together in marriage the two-fold good of love between husband and wife and the good of welcoming new life. Threats to these, and to the good of human life itself, are to be opposed. The family is a school of deepening humanity which depends on husbands, wives, and children each fulfilling their vocation. This is supported by the Church's mission to provide Catholic education. The family, including different generations and relatives, is the foundation of society. The rights of parents and children are to be protected. Following Christ's example, the Church must witness to the mystery of the gift of married and family love which is a source of holiness and joy.

REFLECTION

Why do you think the Church holds the sacrament of marriage to be so important?

How can the Church support spouses and their families in living out their vocation?

How do you understand the Church as a family?

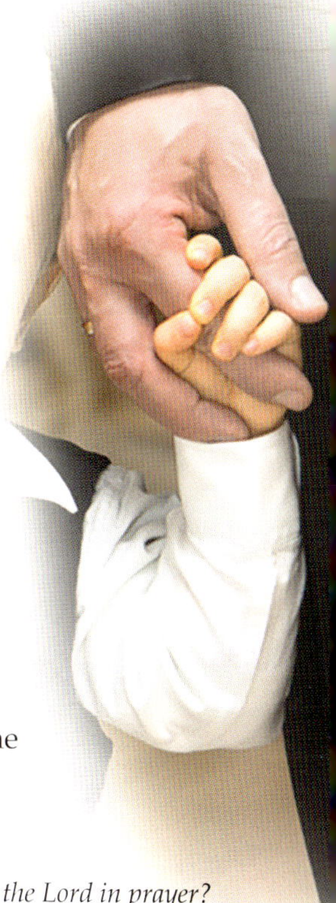

PRAYER

Almighty Father, you created humankind
male and female and established marriage
so that husbands and wives might love each other
and their children. Help all those committed to each other
in marriage to find strength through their faith in Christ,
who blesses this holy sacrament through his Church.
May husbands, wives, and children grow as the Church at home
and be a sign of your love for the world.
We ask this through Christ our Lord. Amen.

In the light of this reflection, is there anything else you would like to bring to the Lord in prayer?

THE PROPER DEVELOPMENT OF CULTURE

(GS 53 – 62)

UNDERSTANDING

Vatican II understands culture as that through which human beings develop and improve the natural and spiritual qualities they have received. Culture is about refining and elevating human gifts for the greater benefit of all. It can also refer to different experiences of how people live in particular communities and traditions. We can, therefore, speak of a variety of cultures, both socially and historically, and we can describe how cultures have developed, both positively and negatively. Vatican II affirms the importance of human beings as agents of culture. We have responsibility for how our existence is enhanced or diminished, both at personal and higher levels. Although competing forces can be at work, we each have a role to play in building a better world. In making their contribution, Christians are guided by their faith which understands humanity and the world in relation to divine truth, and recalls the important relationship between material and spiritual realities. Our vocation is to enhance our appreciation of God's creation, presenting faith in right relationship with reason, science and philosophy.

The Gospel of Christ offers a saving answer to the human condition and shapes human culture which must always serve authentic goods for both individuals and communities. The Church desires to enter into dialogue with the world. By engaging the world with the wisdom of Christ, the Church has a vital role to play towards the progress of culture.

REFLECTION

How do you think you can you best engage with today's culture as a disciple?

How would you describe the culture and society in which you live, and what are some of the blessings and challenges?

What contributions do you think the Church and our faith can make to human progress?

PRAYER

Lord Jesus,
you were born into our world at a particular time and place in history.
You experienced the culture of your own day, as we experience ours.
You brought the Gospel message of God's love and forgiveness which
challenged and changed how people thought and lived, then and now.
May the freshness of your teaching penetrate our minds and hearts anew,
so that we might seek the things that are above, in heaven,
as we live by your commandments on earth. Amen.

In the light of this reflection, is there anything else you would like to bring to the Lord in prayer?

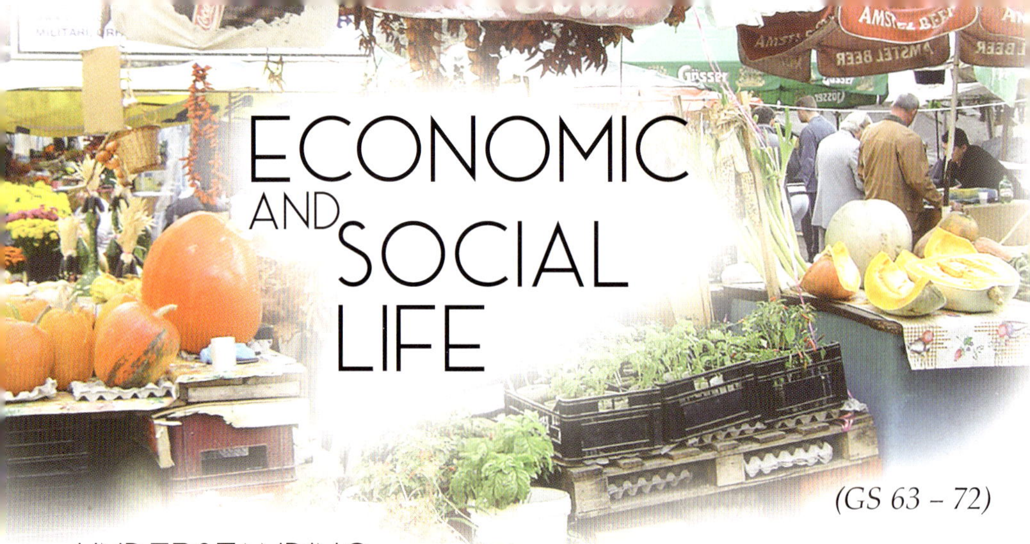

ECONOMIC AND SOCIAL LIFE

(GS 63 – 72)

UNDERSTANDING

Vatican II places the God-given dignity and vocation of the human person at the centre of all economic life (that which relates to trade and industry) and all social life (that which relates to human interaction). Economic life and social life can develop in good and positive ways. They can also increase inequality and injustice, particularly for the weak and the poor. Inequalities of wealth and opportunity can create divisions which, in turn, can threaten peace. To this discussion the Church brings the light of the Gospel, and the tradition of Catholic social teaching, in defence of justice and fairness.

In pursing economic productivity, human and spiritual values must not be overlooked. Development must serve the well-being of the human person, never treating people as mere instruments for profit. Human progress falters under dictatorship or political systems of inequality. Workers have rights, including to union representation; and producers have responsibilities. These must be kept in balance. Progress is important, but cannot be justified when human dignity is devalued. Respecting God's image in each person means securing working conditions and standards that promote human and spiritual values. The earth's resources are to be shared fairly. Investment and property must be managed according to ethical principles to ensure the weak and poor are not disadvantaged. Through the Church, and the witness of Christ's disciples, the Gospel brings to economic and social life the values of God's kingdom.

REFLECTION

In what areas do you think there has been genuine progress in our world in modern times?

How do you think some people might be disadvantaged by the progress of others?

Which key teachings of Christ and the Church do you think are relevant to economic and social life?

PRAYER

Almighty Father, you created the world and entrusted it to humankind,
making us guardians of creation.
You teach us that every person is created in your image.
Your Son, the Lord Jesus, called us to love others, without exception,
and to see and serve him in the weakest and the poorest.
Help us to play our part in building a just society for all,
free of oppression and injustice.
We ask this through Christ our Lord. Amen.

In the light of this reflection, is there anything else you would like to bring to the Lord in prayer?

POLITICAL LIFE

(GS 73 – 76)

UNDERSTANDING

Enormous social changes took place in the nineteenth and twentieth centuries. This brought about different political understandings as to how to organise society, some with devastating consequences for peace and justice. Politics describes systems of government. Some political systems can work to protect and enhance human dignity and rights while others can threaten and destroy them. According to Vatican II, every political system must be based on principles of justice and goodness. Political communities and public authorities are to serve the common good. This means creating and maintaining the necessary social conditions to enable the authentic human development of individuals, families, and communities. There is an important moral order to society which the Church must proclaim and political activity must uphold.

All citizens have a role to play in political life, not least in electing their government. The Church supports those who dedicate themselves to serving the public and the common good. While there can be legitimate political differences concerning policy, the test is always how such policies promote human dignity and values. The Church and political community have different and distinct areas of responsibility, but there can be opportunities for co-operation towards the common good. In this, the Church's primary proclamation always remains the Gospel of Christ's redeeming love.

REFLECTION

In the light of faith, what do you think are some of the primary responsibilities of good government?
How do you understand the proper relationship between the Church and politics?
What teachings of Christ do you think underpin the Church's promotion of the common good?

PRAYER

Heavenly Father,
your Son offers the perfect example of leadership
summarised in his commandment that we love you
and our neighbour.
He called us to live a new kind of community
where concern for the outcast and the stranger,
the poor and the weak,
set the agenda and priority for action.
Help us to work together to create a civilisation
of love where every person is respected
and has the opportunity to flourish.
We ask this through Christ our Lord. Amen.

In the light of this reflection, is there anything else you would like to bring to the Lord in prayer?

AND THE PEACE COMMUNITY OF NATIONS

(GS 77 – 91)

UNDERSTANDING

Vatican II sets before us the teaching of the Lord Jesus that *'Blessed are the peacemakers, for they shall be called children of God.' (Mt 5:9)* The Council condemns war and urges peace, encouraging Christians to do everything possible to build lasting peace in the world. Warfare destroys peace, but true peace is more than a lack of war. With proper regard for God's will, and the Gospel of Christ, the Prince of Peace, true peace means walking together, faithfully and vigilantly, along the path of justice. Nations, governments, and individuals must avoid all that leads to the horror of war, especially given the spectre of nuclear weapons.

There must be clarity about the implications of stockpiling weapons for defence and deterrence, rejecting whatever breeds suspicion and endangers stability. The 'total war,' which obliterates entire cities and their people is condemned outright. Holding weapons for potential use in war does not secure peace. The 'arms race,' costing enormous amounts of money, promotes a mentality of 'mutually assured destruction.' Removing whatever contributes to the possibility of war, and actively promoting peace and disarmament, are necessary tasks for the international community of nations, with a particular concern for developing countries.

The Church, faithful to the Gospel, must witness to human dignity, peace, and solidarity, working with all people of good will to create a peaceful global future for everyone.

REFLECTION

In what ways do you think the Church can promote peace?

How might you make known the importance of peace to politicians and government?

How can you be a peacemaker in your everyday life?

PRAYER

Almighty Father, God of peace,
when your Son rose victorious over death and sin
he offered the world the gift of his peace.
So often we hear of war and violence,
and feel powerless to be peacemakers.
Give us strength, through prayer and witness,
never to be discouraged or complacent about the work for peace in our world.
May hearts of war be transformed by the power of your peace.
We ask this through Christ our Lord. Amen.

In the light of this reflection, is there anything else you would like to bring to the Lord in prayer?

A FINAL REFLECTION

Thank you for making this journey of exploration of the key themes of the four main Constitutions of the Second Vatican Council. There is certainly more to discover in them, and also in the other documents of Vatican II and in secondary writing, interpretation, and resources. Be encouraged to take a next step, whatever that might be for you.

At the close of the Last General Meeting of Vatican II, on 7 December 1965, Pope Paul VI gave an address which included these words:

> "The Church has gathered herself together in deep spiritual awareness, not to produce a learned analysis of religious psychology, or an account of her own experiences, not even to devote herself to reaffirming her rights and explaining her laws. Rather, it was to find in herself, active and alive, the Holy Spirit, the word of Christ; and to probe more deeply still the mystery, the plan and the presence of God above and within herself; to revitalize in herself that faith which is the secret of her confidence and of her wisdom, and that love which impels her to sing without ceasing the praises of God."

May we, members of the Church, Christ's body, continue to be open to the Holy Spirit, to the word of Christ, so that we can sing of God's love to each other and to the world. Amen.

THE SIXTEEN DOCUMENTS OF VATICAN II

Here is a full list of the sixteen documents of Vatican II.

Constitution on the Sacred Liturgy (*Sacrosanctum Concilium*), 4 Dec 1963.

Decree on the Instruments of Social Communication (*Inter Mirifica*), 4 Dec 1963.

Dogmatic Constitution on the Church (*Lumen Gentium*), 21 Nov 1964.

Decree on Ecumenism (*Unitatis Redintegratio*), 21 Nov 1964.

Decree on Eastern Catholic Churches (*Orientalium Ecclesiarum*), 21 Nov 1964.

Decree on the Bishops' Pastoral Office in the Church (*Christus Dominus*), 28 Oct 1965.

Decree on Priestly Formation (*Optatam Totius*), 28 Oct 1965.

Decree on the Appropriate Renewal of the Religious Life (*Perfectae Caritatis*), 28 Oct 1965.

Declaration on the Relationship of the Church to Non-Christian Religions (*Nostra Aetate*), 28 Oct 1965.

Declaration on Christian Education (*Gravissimum Educationis*), 28 Oct 1965.

Dogmatic Constitution on Divine Revelation (*Dei Verbum*), 18 Nov 1965.

Decree on the Apostolate of the Laity (*Apostolicam Actuositatem*), 18 Nov 1965.

Declaration on Religious Freedom (*Dignitatis Humanae*), 7 Dec 1965.

Decree on the Ministry and Life of Priests (*Presbyterorum Ordinis*), 7 Dec 1965.

Decree on the Church's Missionary Activity (*Ad Gentes*), 7 Dec 1965.

Pastoral Constitution on the Church in the Modern World (*Gaudium et Spes*), 7 Dec 1965.